ELEPHANTS

WRITER

Jean Brody

SERIES EDITORS

Vicki León and Joni Hunt

PHOTOGRAPHERS

Frank S. Balthis, Jim Brandenburg, Stanley Breeden,
Dennis Curry, Dr. E.R. Degginger, Gerry Ellis,
Martha Hill, M.P. Kahl, Stephen J. Krasemann, Frans Lanting,
Joe McDonald, Mary Ann McDonald, Robert and Linda Mitchell,
Doug Perrine, Kevin Schafer, Twila Stofer, Kennan Ward, Art Wolfe

DESIGNER

Ashala Nicols Lawler

SILVER BURDETT PRESS

© 1995 Silver Burdett Press
Published by Silver Burdett Press.
A Simon & Schuster Company
299 Jefferson Road, Parsippany, NJ 07054
Printed in the United States of America
10 9 8 7 6 5 4 3 2 1

CLOSE-UP
A Focus on Nature

SILVER BURDETT PRESS
© 1995 Silver Burdett Press
Published by Silver Burdett Press.
A Simon & Schuster Company
299 Jefferson Road, Parsippany, NJ 07054
Printed in the United States of America
10 9 8 7 6 5 4 3 2 1

Library of Congress
Cataloging-in-Publication Data
Brody, Jean.
    Elephants: an affectionate portrait/by Jean
Brody; photographs by Frank S. Balthis . . .
[et al.].
        p.cm. -- (Close up)
    ISBN 0-382-24876-7 (LSB)
    ISBN 0-382-24877-5 (SC)
    1. Elephants--Juvenile literature. [1.
Elephants.] I. Balthis, Frank, ill. II. Title.
III. Series: Close up (Parsippany, N.J.)
QL737.P98B773 1994
599.6'1--dc20   94-30880
                                 CIP
                                 AC

ELEPHANTS

"I have seen a herd of Elephant traveling through dense Native forest...pacing along as if they had an appointment at the end of the world."
— ISAK DINESEN, *OUT OF AFRICA*

WATERING HOLE: Elephants must roam far and wide to find the enormous amounts of food and water they need. They travel migration corridors to follow rains and seasonal foods. Here, African bush elephants share precious water in Botswana.

T IS LATE AFTERNOON. The sun hangs low in the vast African sky. Shadows fall through the fever trees and ride on the rippled surface of a small, clear lake. A hippo lies half submerged in the mud. A sacred ibis and two egrets perch on his back, waiting for him to shift his weight and stir up tidbits for their dinner. Nearby, a herd of Grant's zebras graze. Three giraffes approach the water. Two spread their forelegs and bend to drink. The third waits and watches.

Suddenly, the shadows lengthen, widen, deepen, and become a herd of elephants emerging from the forest. Ears flared and trunks raised, they test the air. The leader – the matriarch – has been coming to this lake for 62 years. As a calf she came with her mother and her mother's family. Now, she brings her own family: her younger sisters, the daughters, and their offspring.

They take the same worn path as did their ancestors in the distant past. Now, as then, they plunge like rightful owners into the water to drink, to bathe, to spray themselves and each other, to entwine their trunks in play and filial affection.

It's no wonder that poet John Donne referred to the elephant as nature's masterpiece, the only harmless great thing.

Elephant lineage

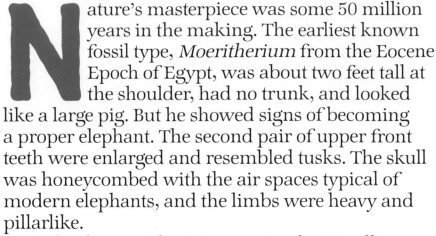

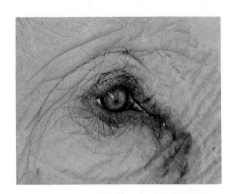

Nature's masterpiece was some 50 million years in the making. The earliest known fossil type, *Moeritherium* from the Eocene Epoch of Egypt, was about two feet tall at the shoulder, had no trunk, and looked like a large pig. But he showed signs of becoming a proper elephant. The second pair of upper front teeth were enlarged and resembled tusks. The skull was honeycombed with the air spaces typical of modern elephants, and the limbs were heavy and pillarlike.

By the dawn of the Miocene Epoch, 35 million years ago, no less than 352 species of the order Proboscidea had spread over most of the earth's surface, occupying such diverse habitats as the far north, the rainforest, and the great plains and savannahs. The late Richard Carrington, who wrote widely on elephants, accounted for this expansion in two ways. Competition forced some members of a population to seek greener pastures, a natural evolutionary process known as adaptative radiation. But Dr. Carrington also believed that the proboscideans, like some humans, possessed an insatiable wanderlust. He called them "daring animal explorers."

It was a mere five million years ago that *Elephantidae*, the family to which today's African and Asian elephants belong, appears in the fossil record. This family produced 30 species, some of which were around long enough to be hunted to extinction by our own ancestors. The story of man and elephant as predator and prey goes back at least 50,000 years. Evidence is found in cave paintings and crudely worked ivory. Even so, most paleontologists agree that the great dying off of the proboscidean dynasty was caused not by man, but by changes in the earth's climate and subsequent shortages of food and water.

From the earliest days of domestication in Asia, around 2,000 B.C., the elephant was used in warfare.

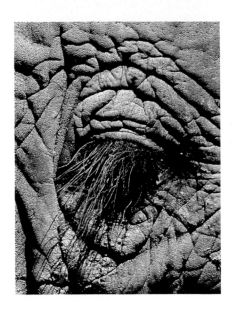

SKIN DEEP: Why are elephants wrinkled like prunes? Wrinkles store moisture. The eye of an African elephant, lower photo, has deep wrinkles and thick eyelashes to protect it from the hot, dry climate. An Asian elephant, top, lives in moister places. Which kind of elephant is eating grass at right?

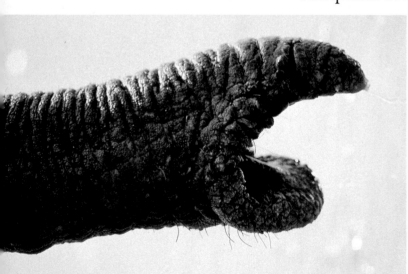

This practice spread to the West as a result of the conquests of Alexander the Great. The most famous elephant troops in history are the 37 animals that set out from Spain with Hannibal in 219 B.C. According to zoo historian Robert Delort, they crossed the Pyrenees, swam and rafted the Rhone, and finally scaled the Alps without a single loss. In northwest Italy, on the banks of the snow-swept Trebia River, Hannibal defeated the Romans. Coins struck to commemorate the event indicate that both African and Asian elephants were used in the campaign. After Trebia, the elephants died off, probably from extreme cold and starvation. One-eyed Hannibal is said to have ridden the lone survivor, a one-tusked Asian elephant named Surus.

Even in our own time, elephants have gone to war. During World War II, the British and Indian armies used them for transport and bridge building. In Vietnam the Viet Cong used them to move supplies. American helicopter gun crews were ordered to shoot them on sight.

Most people today know the elephant as work animal and entertainer. Even in our mechanized world, they are still gainfully employed in the timber industry in Asia. The role of entertainer dates back to the Roman games where they were pitted against bulls and gladiators. In a precursor to the modern circus, they were trained to dance, to walk tightropes, to spread flowers and even to sit down to a banquet in the middle of the arena. The Roman naturalist and writer Pliny tells of an elephant that was beaten because it did not learn quickly enough to suit its trainer. One night it was found practicing the routine – all alone.

In 1882, Jumbo, the most celebrated of elephants, was bought by P.T. Barnum for $10,000 from the London Zoo. The sale caused a national scandal and was debated in Parliament. News of Jumbo's death when he was struck by a train made the newspaper headlines all over the world.

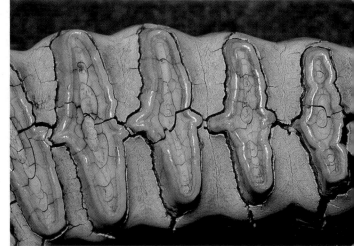

What is an elephant?

An old myth from India tells of six blind men, reputed to be wise, who joined forces in an attempt to determine the nature of the elephant. The question was, "What is it?" The first blind man tripped and fell against the elephant's side, crying out, "It is a wall!" The second felt a tusk and said it was a spear. The third took hold of the trunk and said it was none other than a great snake. The fourth felt its leg and called it a tree. The fifth touched an ear and said it

TRANSFORMER TRUNK: Much of what an elephant does, it does with its trunk, lower left. Some 60,000 muscles work to feed, shower, trumpet, and snorkel. It can also be a straw, sucking water up and blowing it out, top left.

Because an elephant's teeth are so large, only four are in use at once. A single tooth, above, has flat, vertical plates for chewing. A nine-month old has only 1½ square inches of chewing area; a 45-year old has up to 50. Teeth help to estimate age.

was a fan. The sixth seized the tail and proclaimed it a rope. They argued far into the night.

Had a seventh blind man come along, one truly wise, he might have run his hands over the whole animal and come closer to the truth. First he would have remarked on the great size. Largest of the living land mammals, the African weighs around seven tons, the Asian six – give or take a few hundred pounds. (It's no easy task to weigh an elephant.) Record height is 13 feet, 2 inches at the shoulder in an African bull. Average is 11 feet in the African, 10 feet in the Asian. Males in both cases are larger than females.

An animal this massive clearly needs something substantial to move around on. The leg is pillarlike. The upper limb bones are longer than the lower, an arrangement that gives support rather than speed. Even so, an elephant with its long stride can "fast-walk" at more than 15 miles per hour.

When you look at an elephant skeleton in a museum, you see that the animal is up on the balls of its feet, with the heel carried off the ground

BY ANY OTHER NAME:
An African elephant, left, has ears shaped like its home continent and two "fingers" at the end of its trunk. Both sexes grow tusks.

Spraying its keeper or mahout, above, the smaller Asian elephant has ears shaped like India, a one-fingered trunk, and two bumps atop its head. Only 60 percent of the males grow tusks. Some lose skin pigment from trunks and ears.

UNLIKELY KIN: As strange as it seems, an elephant's closest living relatives are the manatee, above, and dugong, which live in tropical waters, and the furry hyrax, right, which is about the size of a guinea pig. Some 50 million years ago they shared a common ancestor. Today dugongs and manatees, like elephants, are endangered.

in a position called digitigrade. In the living elephant, a wedge-shaped pad of elastic tissue supports and cushions the heel. The pad spreads weight evenly and accounts for the elephant's sure-footedness and remarkably soft tread.

An elephant tusk, which the blind man mistook for a spear, is at times used as a weapon but is primarily a tool for food gathering. In the African, both sexes have tusks. About 40 percent of Asian males are tuskless, and they are barely visible in females. Tusks, or modified incisors, are composed entirely of dentine, also known as ivory. Record length is 11.4 feet for the right one and 11 feet for the left in an African bull. Just as we are right or left-handed, elephants are right- or left- tusked, with the dominant side showing more signs of wear. The heaviest-known tusks together weighed 460 pounds when they were collected. The average today is about 13 pounds.

Molars erupt in grooves rather than in sockets as ours do. They form in succession – like a production line – and migrate forward, pushing out the worn predecessors. Only four molars, of the lifetime supply of 24, are in use at one time. Each set of four is larger and lasts longer than the previous one. The last set come in at around age 30 and will last for another 30 years or so. An elephant in its 60s is grinding on its last set of teeth.

The skin appears baggy and ill-fitting, but the wrinkles are functional. They harbor water and mud and help cool the body. In the African elephant, the wrinkles are deeper than the Asian's, an adaptation to the arid environment.

The ears, too, act as a temperature regulator, particularly the larger ears of the African. In the heat of the day the animal extends them and faces downwind, or flaps them to produce its own breeze. (The fifth blind man was right – the ear is a fan!) Near the skin surface on the back of the ear lies an intricate network of blood vessels. Here, the hot blood carried by the arteries is cooled before it returns to

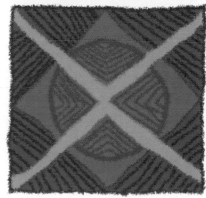

the body through the veins. At night the ears are held close to the head to conserve body heat.

Iain Douglas-Hamilton, a Scots zoologist, used the back of the ears as a means of identification. He photographed the network of vessels, which are as singular as fingerprints and change little over the years.

Elephants "talk" with their ears. The matriarch signals her family when it's time to rest or feed or move on by flapping them against her neck and shoulders, then letting them slide down. She warns of threats by folding each ear to form a horizontal ridge across the middle. Family members and bond groups greet each other by lifting and spreading the ears, then flapping them wildly.

The trunk, which the third blind man likened to a snake, is an elongation of the upper lip and nose. Nostrils are located at the tip, along with one (Asian) or two (African) fingerlike appendages. The trunk is operated by approximately 60,000 muscles, and the tip is so sensitive it can pluck a single flower. Ancient elephants were small and stumpy, but with progressive increase in size the head moved farther from the ground. In other animals that grew to great heights – the giraffe for example – the problem was solved by elongating the neck. But elephants were already committed to large heads to support

DUSTING POWDER: Unlike humans, elephants play in the dirt <u>after</u> they've taken a bath. They suck up dirt with their trunks, and blow it onto their wet bodies so it sticks well. Although the name 'pachyderm' means thick-skinned, their skin is sensitive to heat, dryness, and insects. These elephants in Namibia take on the reddish hue from minerals in the dirt.

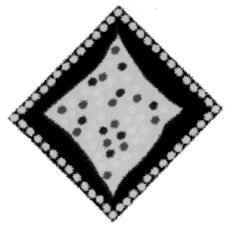

MUDDERS: Elephants often wallow in the mud for hours, like the family above. On especially hot days, they may flap their ears like fans to create a cooling breeze, right.

their heavy tusks and trunks. Lengthening the neck would have put such a strain on the muscles that the head would have been unmanageable. The most practical solution was for nature to fill the gap between the head and the ground by stretching the snout. *Voilà!* A trunk!

An elephant uses its trunk to swat flies, pick up grass, slap mud on itself to keep cool, and sing to itself down the length of it. Some other uses: to dig for water, strip bark, take dust baths, greet friends, snorkle while swimming, and smell out the situation. It's also used as a hose for drinking, a trumpet to announce displeasure, and a hand for helping babies up the bank.

In the service of man, the trunk is logger, loader, and builder. For man's pleasure, elephants have been trained to take tickets, pick up coins, uncork bottles, and play the piano. There's even elephant art!

In 1982, drawings were submitted to Jerome Witkin, an authority on abstract expressionism. He called the drawings "lyrical," and said whoever did them was versed in Eastern calligraphy. The artist

was from the Far East – a 14-year-old elephant from Thailand known as Siri.

When David Gucwa became Siri's keeper in 1980, he noticed how she used pebbles to make what he perceived as drawings on the floor of her enclosure. He gave her heavy paper and a carpenter's pencil to work with. Some 200 drawings later, Siri became a celebrity. As a result, other zoos and circuses offered up their own elephant artists. There was spirited speculation from philosophers and behaviorists about the "meaning" of these artistic creations. Did elephants think? Was the art an expression of higher intelligence? Do elephants have feelings? Souls even? As with the wise men, there was much discussion but little consensus. One keeper at the Toronto Zoo summed it up. "...You can divide all mammals into three basic groups: you've got your humans, you've got your elephants, and then you've got everything else."

Life cycle

Breeding and birth can take place year round. After a pregnancy of up to 22 months, one calf is born. Newborns weigh as much as 265 pounds and are about three feet tall at the shoulder. Sexual maturity occurs between ages 10 and 14 in females and as late as 17 in males. At puberty the male leaves the family and joins a bachelor band. Females tend to remain for life with the group into which they were born.

A type of natural birth control can be observed in times of drought or other environmental stress. Maturity is delayed in juveniles and females cease to be fertile. One study found that the age of puberty was related to population density. In Tanzania where there were two to three elephants per square mile, the mean age of sexual maturity was 12 years. In

LOOKING HIGH AND LOW: During a single day, an adult eats about 300 pounds of food, foraging up to 19 hours. Along with grasses, roots, and fruits, elephants eat nutrient-rich trees. They tear off branches and leaves, left, and strip bark. If leaves are out of reach, they may knock over a tree, as with the baobab, above.

Uganda, however, with six to ten elephants per square mile, puberty was reached at age 22.

In ideal conditions a female can bear her first calf at 12 and continue to produce offspring every four years until she enters menopause sometime in her 50s. Both sexes can live to 70, but by this time they are chewing on the remnants of their last molars and suffering from malnutrition and the ailments of old age.

For years, tales told by early explorers about the behavior of elephants in the presence of death were dismissed as ravings of men who'd spent too much time in the bush. Now, researchers have photographic evidence. Typically, a member of the herd succumbs to accident, illness, old age, or human predation. The family mills around in obvious distress. They scream and trumpet, try to lift the stricken animal or bring it food and water in their trunks. After hours of vigil they may cover the body with dirt or branches, then

ELEPHANT WALK: In their continual search for food and water, elephants travel trails trod by their ancestors. Desert dwellers, like this family in Namibia, may travel 30 miles between a food source and water. When surface water is gone, the matriarch uses her experience to locate water and dig wells.

slowly move on. Iain Douglas-Hamilton wrote: "I have no doubt that when one of their number dies and the bonds of a lifetime are severed, elephants have a similar feeling to the one we call grief."

Perhaps they also feel rage. In Tanzania, a bull was shot and left to rot so it would be easier to collect the ivory. Elephants were seen carrying off the tusks, which were later found smashed against rocks. In Uganda, a herd broke into a shed where game croppers had stored ears and feet to be marketed as handbags and umbrella stands. They took them away and covered them with leaves.

George Adamson wrote of a bull that was shot while raiding a garden. The meat was given to the local people and the remains dragged about a half mile away. That night elephants returned the shoulder blade and a leg bone to the exact spot where the bull was shot.

Elephant behaviors

One of the reasons these stories are credible is furnished by the intricate structure of elephant society itself. The basic grouping is known as the family unit. Composed of related females and their offspring, it usually numbers around ten individuals. The unit is led by a matriarch, the oldest and therefore the largest, strongest, and presumably wisest female.

The second level of organization is the kinship or bond group, family units that maintain contact with each other. Rowan Martin, a researcher, introduced another level – that of the clan – with as many as 100 members that associate with each other but not neighboring clans. Adult males live either alone or in loose bands called bull herds.

An elephant can spend up to 19 hours a day eating. Grass is the principal food during the wet season; browse, including leaves, twigs, and shrubs, during the dry times. The matriarch, who knows where and when food is plentiful, leads her family along

established routes. She determines where and when they will feed, rest, and drink. If water is available, an elephant will consume up to 40 gallons a day. However, the African has shown the capacity to go without for extended periods. One herd of 34 was trapped in an enclosure for two weeks. All but two juveniles survived the experience. The desert elephants of Skeleton Coast Park in Namibia sometimes go four days between water holes.

In 1984 at the Washington Park Zoo in Oregon, biologist Katherine Payne watched three Asian elephants and their calves. She noticed a "throbbing in the air like distant thunder." Later she recalled that as a choir girl her place was next to the largest organ pipe in the church. On the low notes the whole chapel would throb. She wondered if that "distant thunder"

SPARRING PARTNERS: Two youngsters play-fight in Kenya. Like most juvenile animals, elephants play often to test and develop the skills they'll use later as adults. Larger siblings will drop to their knees to even the match when playing with smaller ones.

she had felt in Portland came from the elephants. Were they communicating in a range too low-pitched for the human ear? A few months later she and two colleagues returned to the zoo to test this theory. Electronic printouts of recordings proved that the majority of elephant calls fell into that low-frequency range called infrasound.

The following year Payne and her colleagues studied elephant calls in Kenya's Ambroseli National Park and in Namibia. With video and sophisticated recording equipment they documented long-distance infrasonic communication and found that family units keep contact with each other over a distance of at least 2½ miles. Females were generally more "talkative" than males, a fact presumed to be more related to social structure than gender.

What do they "talk" about? Like members of human families, elephants call to each other about

CLOSE TO YOU: Even the largest and strongest land mammals – at six to eight tons – snuggle. Elephants of all ages are social and interact frequently. They huddle in groups, caress each other, and entwine trunks, left. From the rear, elephants with their loose and wrinkly skin look as if they're wearing baggy pants, above.

UNDERFOOT: Female elephants bear young, called calves, about once every four years. The hairy newborns stay in their mother's shadow and receive lots of TLC, plus their mother's milk, and her protection from hungry lions and hyenas.

HOW TO HANDLE A TRUNK: A calf shakes its head and watches the trunk wiggle. It sucks it like a human baby sucks its thumb. Instead of sipping through the trunk at a water hole, a calf kneels to drink with its mouth. Sometimes a baby even trips over it. Finally at about five months old, a calf sucks up water and blows it out. With practice, it begins to hit targets more often than it misses.

food, water, and danger. And perhaps – like us – sometimes just to chat. Also, male bulls learn the location of receptive females, called cows. In one experiment workers played an infrasonic recording of a female in heat to two bulls at the water hole. The bulls immediately set out for the direction of the van that housed the equipment.

Because the sexes do not travel together and a female may be fertile for as few as two days every four years, infrasonic communication helps bring breeding pairs together. Once a year healthy bull elephants over 30 come into a condition called *musth*, or rut, characterized by high sex hormone levels, aggression towards other males, and intense interest in females. The musth bull calls frequently, secretes a sticky fluid from swollen temporal glands on the sides of his head, and leaves a trail of strong-smelling urine. The penis may turn a greenish color, a fact noted but not understood by observers.

Typically, the arrival of the suitor is preceded by a sharp acrid odor. He approaches the family unit with head held high, chin tucked in, ears waving.

All the females and calves, in addition to the cow in heat, appear to treat his presence as a time for celebration. There is much milling about and touching of trunks. Then the cow "runs away," followed by the bull, whose courtship consists of running his trunk over her back.

After a brief mating, the cow rumbles and the family comes running. They flap their ears, scream, trumpet, and extend their trunks to touch the pair in what has been called a "mating pandemonium." The consortship may last for another two days or so with or without another mating.

Remarkably, few mortal battles over breeding rights are recorded. High-ranking bulls appear to avoid each other by use of urine trails and infrasound. Low-ranking males simply give way when a musth bull appears on the scene. Most breeding is accomplished by males over 35. Studies show that females appear to prefer older bulls. Not only will the offspring inherit genes of experienced adults, but the presence of an older bull discourages young males that harass females in a breeding condition. Musth lasts two to three months and leaves the bull weary and thin.

Because so few elephant births are observed in the wild, information on the process is scanty. Sometimes the expectant mother leaves her group and gives birth alone, but examples exist of birth taking place with the family present.

In her book, *Elephant Memories*, Cynthia Moss, who conducted a 14-year study in Ambroseli National Park, gives detailed accounts of the two births observed during the study. In both instances the mother gave birth standing up and was attended by members of her family.

Deborah, a 47-year-old experienced mother, appeared competent from the moment the calf was born. After 1½ hours, the young suckled from its mother, and a short time later from an "auntie."

In sharp contrast, Tullulah, who at 17 was giving birth for the first time, appeared upset and confused. She was clumsy as she tried to remove the fetal sac and didn't know how to lift the calf when it toppled over. Nor did she position herself so it could reach her teat. Over four hours passed before the infant nursed successfully.

In Tullulah's defense, Moss pointed out that it had been several years since a calf had been born into her family. Both she and the young female that attended her hadn't had the opportunity to learn mothering by example. Despite this shaky start, Tullulah got the hang of it and her calf thrived.

MATERNAL CARE: Female elephants – whether mother or aunt – lavish attention on calves. The young ones often need a nudge climbing a steep bank, above, or help leaving a mud hole. A baby's squeals bring adults running. The mother at right simplifies nursing for her calf by keeping one leg forward.

The first few months of a calf's life is spent in constant association with its mother. It suckles until around age three but meanwhile learns, by trial and error, to use its trunk to eat and drink. Adults are attentive and indulgent. If a calf decides to stop and take a nap, the family waits patiently until the baby is ready to move on. Visiting bulls are tolerant of the playful advances of the young. Adolescent females "babysit" the calves. Orphans have been successfully fostered onto unrelated families. In John F. Eisenberg's study of Ceylon elephants, he found that the mere presence of several infants could produce milk in females that had no nursing young of their own.

Many researchers believe that the solicitous, mindful behavior of the family, in part, accounts for the longevity of elephants. Because of the protection furnished by the herd, few calves and juveniles fall victim to natural predators. They reach a size and age where their only significant enemy is man.

Elephants & man

Elephants have been killed for their ivory since the first Stone Age hunter discovered that mammoth tusks lent themselves to whittling. Archaeologists found remains of an ivory shop on Crete, dated at 1450 B.C. Both Tutankhamen and King Solomon sat on ivory thrones and drank from ivory goblets. In ancient Rome, ivory beds, tables, and even floors were status symbols. The favorite horse of notorious Roman Emperor Caligula ate from an ivory manger.

By the 10th century Arab traders established centers in east Africa from which they supplied carvers in China. In the 15th century, the Portuguese were trading in both tusks and the slaves who carried them to the coast. This practice continued well into the 19th century. In the early 1900s an estimated

50,000 elephants were slaughtered each year. The European governments that ruled Africa became alarmed and enacted game laws. The Society of the Friends of the Elephant was founded in Paris "...to stop the terrible annual slaughter...."

But reprieve for the elephants came not from legislation nor good intentions. It came from the two wars which claimed the world's energy and attention, and it was short-lived.

Uganda furnishes a vivid example of the decline that followed World War II. By 1966 the expanding human population had pushed 8,000 elephants into a small section of one of the parks. Less than 10 years later, the rising price of ivory and the poaching that resulted reduced the numbers to 1,700. In 1980, in the chaos that followed the fall of Idi Amin, troops and poachers with automatic weapons brought the total to 160.

It was the same story over much of Africa. The mythical elephant graveyards had become a grim reality. Even so, the African elephant was not granted endangered status by CITES (The Convention on

IN CHARGE: Because of its great size, an adult male has few enemies other than rival elephants and man. When threatened, it approaches the rival, nods its head, and holds its ears out to make its head look larger, left. The next step is to charge, above. Rivals rarely fight to the death.

International Trade in Endangered Species). The Asian elephant, whose population is much smaller than the African's, was declared endangered in 1975. But because females and a large percentage of males are tuskless, there is no immediate threat to the Asians' survival. At least not from ivory fever.

In 1985, CITES initiated the Ivory Export Quota System. Member nations agreed to quotas based on keeping the elephant populations healthy and then followed prescribed procedures for export and import. But in June 1988, Iain Douglas-Hamilton testified in Washington that the system was a failure. He said, "I only know that when I fly surveys, each time I find fewer elephants alive, and thousands of carcasses...."

On July 17, 1989, the desperate nature of the elephant's plight was seen all over the world on the evening news. President Daniel Moi of Kenya stood in front of 13 tons of elephant tusks and said, "Great objectives require great sacrifices. I now call upon the people of the world to join us in Kenya by eliminating the trade in ivory once and for all." He then put a torch to

UNCOVERING THE GOODS: Cattle egrets on an elephant's back snatch up insects stirred from the grass as the elephant forages, above. Tusks come in handy for digging minerals like iron from the soil, right, digging roots, and prying bark off trees. Although they grow 3½ to 4½ inches a year, tusks reach only half their potential length because of wear and breakage.

a gasoline-drenched mountain of poached tusks. Newspapers and magazines carried stories and grizzly photographs of the unrelenting carnage, which from 1979 to 1989 brought the elephant population of Africa from 1.3 million to 625,000.

The following October, CITES met in Switzerland to determine whether or not the African elephant would be declared endangered and a worldwide ban placed on the sale of ivory. Countries like South Africa and Zimbabwe, where poaching was strictly controlled, populations kept in check by culling, and meat and tusks marketed to the benefit of the economy, argued they should not be punished because other countries couldn't manage their own households. After a heated debate, on October 17, 1989, temporary endangered status for African elephants was approved by a vote of 76 to 11.

All the member nations agreed that poaching is reprehensible. Debate centered – as it does today – on culling and the necessity for it. In southern Africa culls are conducted by specialists – marksmen who can take out an entire family in 90 seconds. Pro-cullers contend it is more humane to remove whole herds rather than select for breeding females. Anti-cullers say this practice could wipe out genetic lines and result in inbreeding. Many add that culling simply isn't ethical.

Some wildlife managers maintain that because elephants destroy their own habitat, culling is necessary to keep the ecosystem healthy and stable. Anti-cullers see woodland decline and renewal as part of a long-term natural cycle. They point to studies that show how elephants open up impenetrable thickets and promote growth of plants used by other species. How, in their wanderings they disperse seed pods in their dung, and during droughts dig wells that are used by animals and humans alike.

Even if compromises in management methods

PRECIOUS COMMODITY: In the 1970s, the sale of a single elephant's tusks equaled 12 years of labor to a subsistence farmer in Africa. Ivory became an illegal currency, and poaching became commonplace. As the largest-tusked elephants were killed, poachers shot younger ones. In 1988, twice as many elephants were killed to collect one ton of ivory as were in 1979.

are reached, even if poaching is brought completely under control, and even if ivory becomes passé, both African and Asian elephants face another formidable foe – the rising human population and the need for land and food to sustain it. Most specialists agree that in addition to sanctuaries and reserves, elephants need corridors between ranges so they can follow their food supply. If they encounter fences and croplands, they destroy them. Planned open corridors that consider these ancient migratory routes could help solve part of the problem.

As for the world's lust for ivory, recently the first "test-tube" variety was developed in Japan. Whipped up primarily from eggs and milk, it can be used to make everything from billiard balls to utensils for a Japanese tea party.

Substitutes for ivory are nothing new. In the early part of this century, Colombia and Ecuador exported tons of tagua – a nut from an Amazonian palm tree – to Europe where it was carved into such items as chess pieces, jewelry, dice, and buttons. It was much in demand until plastics came on the market. Now, tagua is making a comeback. A female tagua tree produces about 20 pounds of nuts a year, approximately the amount of ivory on a female elephant. And it goes on producing after each harvest. It's also a boon to severely threatened rainforests as a renewable resource that can generate five times the income of banana plantations or cattle ranches.

For people who insist on the "real thing," mammoth tusks are the answer. Buried in the permafrost of Siberia are vast deposits of mammoth ivory, which is indistinguishable to the naked eye

DOMESTIC HELP: Records from India show elephants were domesticated about 2,000 B.C. Today they parade in festivals, left, and work in logging camps, above. Elephants respond to their mahout's verbal commands and prods. Ironically, elephants hauling timber aid deforestation and the destruction of their own habitat.

from that of elephants. Such rich fields of fossil ivory are also believed to exist in North America.

Living, breathing elephants, too, can be a significant source of income. Tourists are among their best friends. In Asia, visitors pay handsomely to ride elephants in the jungle and watch them in ceremonies. In Africa, elephants along with rhinos and the big cats are major attractions. A survey in Kenya showed that elephants alone bring in about $200 million annually in tourist dollars. It's estimated that an elephant is worth over $14,000 a year for every year it lives – a potential value of $900,000 to the Kenyan economy.

It appears that if people can learn to coexist with elephants, the elephant can pay its own way. Of course, that is easy to say if you live in a country where elephants are kept in zoos and wild animal parks, and your own garden is in no danger. Responding to criticism from a visitor from the West, an official of the Zimbabwe Trust said, "Did you 'protect' your bears or your wolves when you were developing agriculture?" Problems and solutions – like elephants – come not in black and white but in shades of gray.

The temporary worldwide ban on the sale of ivory was still in place in mid-1993. Poaching, however, continues, as does illegal trade. And the human birthrate continues relentlessly on its upward spiral.

In only ten short years, 1979 to 1989, the elephant population was cut in half. The awesome possibility exists that they could become extinct in the coming century. Their fate – and ours as the self-appointed caretakers of the green planet – rests uneasily in our hands.

ABOUT THE AUTHOR

Jean Brody lectures on elephants to the Provisional Docent Class at the Los Angeles Zoo. The characters in her novels are often winged or four-footed. Her short story, "Ivory," appeared in *Lear's*. She lives and writes in Cambria, California.

ABOUT THE PHOTOGRAPHERS

Frank S. Balthis: pages 35, 36 inset
Jim Brandenburg/Minden Pictures: pages 12-13, 22-23
Stanley Breeden/DRK Photo: page 29
Dennis Curry: pages 25, 32
Dr. E. R. Degginger: pages 17, 33
Gerry Ellis: page 28
M. P. Kahl/DRK Photo: page 6 lower photo, 7, 14, 34
Stephen J. Krasemann/DRK Photo: pages 21, 26-27
Frans Lanting/Minden Pictures: pages ii-iii, 2-3, 8, 15, 36-37, 46
Joe McDonald: front cover, pages i, 9, 42
Mary Ann McDonald: pages 16, 31
Robert and Linda Mitchell: page 4 upper photo, 38, 39
Doug Perrine/DRK Photo: page 10
Kevin Schafer and Martha Hill: page 4 lower photo, back cover
Twila Stofer: page 24
Kennan Ward: pages 5, 11, 40-41
Art Wolfe: page 6 upper photo, 18-19, 30

SPECIAL THANKS

Linda Countryman, Greater Los Angeles Zoo Association

TO LEARN MORE

■ African Wildlife Foundation, 1717 Massachusetts Avenue NW, Washington, DC 20036
■ World Wildlife Fund, 1250 24th Street NW, Washington, DC 20037

Books
■ *Elephant Memories*, by Cynthia Moss (Morrow, 1988)
■ *Elephants*, by Peter Jackson (Book Sales, Inc., 1990)
■ *Life and Lore of the Elephant*, by Robert Delort (Abrams, 1990)
■ *Sacred Elephant*, by Heathcote Williams (Harmony Books, 1989)

Films
■ *African Wildlife* (National Geographic)
■ *Elephant* (Silent Safari Series, Britannica Films, 1972, 11 min.)
■ *The Elephant* (Luceren Media, 1981, 21 min.)
■ *Elephants* (Zoo Animals in the Wild Series, Coronet/MTI Film & Video, 1981, 5 min.)
■ *National Geographic: Elephant* (Live Home Video, 1989, 60 min.)
■ *Sierra Club Series: We Live with Elephants* (Kodak, 60 min.)
■ *Wildlife in Action* (World Safari)

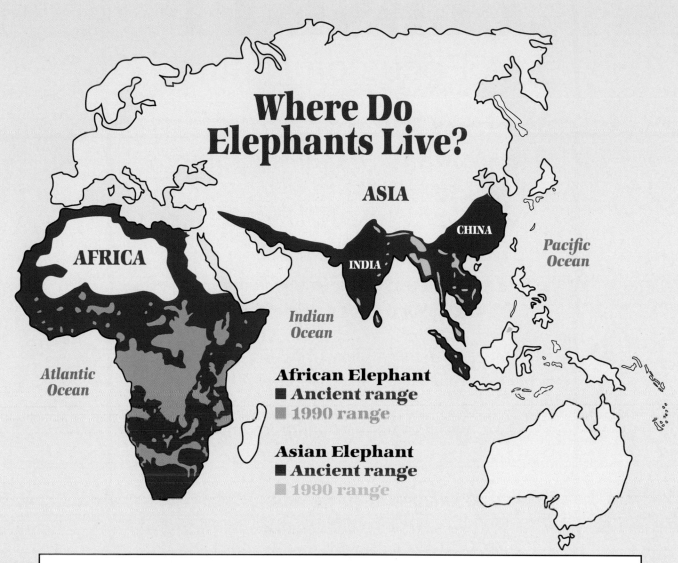

Where Do Elephants Live?

ASIA

CHINA

INDIA

AFRICA

Pacific Ocean

Indian Ocean

Atlantic Ocean

African Elephant
■ Ancient range
■ 1990 range

Asian Elephant
■ Ancient range
■ 1990 range

HOW ELEPHANTS DIFFER

AFRICAN		ASIAN	
Height	Males to 11'	Height	Males to 10'
Weight	7 tons	Weight	6 tons
Tusks	6-8' (record: 11.4')	Tusks	4-5' (male only)
Forehead	Flat	Forehead	Twin-domed
Back	Concave	Back	Convex
Trunk	Two fingers	Trunk	One finger
Nails	5 forefoot, 3 hind	Nails	5 forefoot, 4 hind
Ears	Shaped like continent of Africa	Ears	Shaped like continent of India
Molars	10 plates	Molars	20 or more plates

African elephants are divided into two subspecies, bush and forest.
The forest elephants are smaller, have straighter tusks, and more rounded ears.

CLOSE-UP
A Focus on Nature

Here's what teachers, parents, kids, and nature lovers of all ages say about this series:

• • • • • • • •

"High-interest topics, written in grownup language yet clear enough for kids..."

"Dazzling, detailed photos. Your beautiful books have a strong educational component—keep it up!"

"Packed with facts and priced right for busy adults."

"Extremely useful for students with reading difficulties..."

"Your book is the best souvenir we could have of our whale-watching trip."

"These books are great gift items for all the bird-watchers, divers, and wildlife artists on my list!"

Silver Burdett Press books are widely available at bookstores and gift outlets at museums, zoos, and aquaria throughout the U.S. and abroad. Educators and individuals wishing to order may also do so by writing directly to:

SILVER BURDETT PRESS
299 JEFFERSON ROAD, PARSIPPANY, NJ 07054

HABITATS

The Desert
Hot & dry, but it's home to big cats, camels, coyotes, & more

The KELP FOREST
The ebb and flow of life in the sea's richest habitat

Life at the Frozen Edge
ICEBERGS AND GLACIERS

Tropical RAINFORESTS

Coral Reefs

Tidepools
THE BRIGHT WORLD OF THE ROCKY SHORELINE

BIRDS IN THE WILD

HAWKS, OWLS & OTHER Birds of Prey

PARROTS, MACAWS & COCKATOOS

A dazzle of Hummingbirds

ANIMALS BIG & SMALL

BEARS

Insects
All about ants, aphids, bees, fleas, termites, toebiters, & a beetle or two

A CHORUS OF FROGS

ELEPHANTS

165 million years of DINOSAURS
ALL ABOUT TRICERATOPS, SAUROPODS AND A T-REX OR TWO

Butterflies
Monarchs, moths & more — up close & unexpected

MARINE LIFE

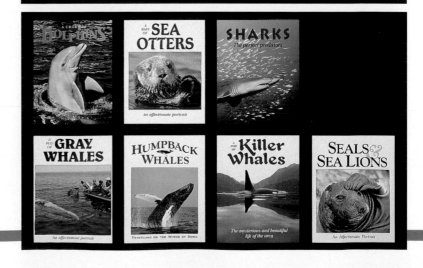

A CHARM OF DOLPHINS

A RAFT OF SEA OTTERS
An affectionate portrait

SHARKS
The perfect predators

A POD OF GRAY WHALES
An affectionate portrait

HUMPBACK WHALES
TRAVELING ON THE WINGS OF SONG

A POD OF Killer WHALES
The mysterious and beautiful life of the orca

SEALS & SEA LIONS
An Affectionate Portrait

"If the great beasts are gone, man would surely die of a great loneliness of spirit."
— Chief Seattle, Duwamish Tribe